ENGINEERING MARVELS

BUILDING THE

GOLDEN GATE BRIDGE

ELSIE OLSON

Consulting Editor, Diane Craig, M.A./Reading Specialist

Super Sandcastle

An Imprint of Abdo Publishing
abdopublishing.com

abdopublishing.com

Published by Abdo Publishing, a division of ABDO, PO Box 398166, Minneapolis, Minnesota 55439. Copyright © 2018 by Abdo Consulting Group, Inc. International copyrights reserved in all countries. No part of this book may be reproduced in any form without written permission from the publisher. Super SandCastle™ is a trademark and logo of Abdo Publishing.

Printed in the United States of America, North Mankato, Minnesota
062017
092017

Editor: Rebecca Felix
Content Developer: Mighty Media, Inc.
Cover and Interior Design and Production: Mighty Media, Inc.
Photo Credits: Alamy; AP Images; Getty Images; iStockphoto; Library of Congress; National Park Service; San Francisco History Center, San Francisco Public Library; Shutterstock; Wikimedia Commons

Publisher's Cataloging-in-Publication Data

Names: Olson, Elsie, author.
Title: Building the Golden Gate Bridge / by Elsie Olson.
Description: Minneapolis, MN : Abdo Publishing, 2018. | Series: Engineering marvels.
Identifiers: LCCN 2016962884 | ISBN 9781532111112 (lib. bdg.) | ISBN 9781680788969 (ebook)
Subjects: LCSH: Golden Gate Bridge (San Francisco, Calif.)– Juvenile literature. | Suspension bridges–Design and construction–Juvenile literature. | Structural engineering–Juvenile literature.
Classification: DDC 624–dc23
LC record available at http://lccn.loc.gov/2016962884

Super SandCastle™ books are created by a team of professional educators, reading specialists, and content developers around five essential components—phonemic awareness, phonics, vocabulary, text comprehension, and fluency—to assist young readers as they develop reading skills and strategies and increase their general knowledge. All books are written, reviewed, and leveled for guided reading, early reading intervention, and Accelerated Reader™ programs for use in shared, guided, and independent reading and writing activities to support a balanced approach to literacy instruction.

CONTENTS

WHAT IS A BRIDGE?

A bridge is a structure that crosses over something. It can carry cars, trains, and people. Bridges cross over water, valleys, and even cities. The Golden Gate Bridge is a famous bridge. It crosses part of the Pacific Ocean.

THE GOLDEN GATE BRIDGE

LOCATION: San Francisco, California

BUILDING STARTED: January 5, 1933

BUILDING COMPLETED: May 27, 1937

CHIEF ENGINEER: Joseph Strauss

LENGTH: 4,200 feet (1,280 m)

HEIGHT: 265 feet (81 m) above water

ROOM TO GROW

In the early 1900s, many people came to California. San Francisco was one of the state's largest cities. But the city had water on three sides. It had no room to grow. There was open land nearby. But it was across a **strait** from the city. City leaders wanted to build a bridge across this strait.

More than half a million people lived in San Francisco by 1920.

The bridge would allow San Francisco to grow. But such a bridge would not be easy to build.

A TRICKY STRAIT

The **strait** is known as the Golden Gate. It connects the Pacific Ocean to the San Francisco Bay. Strong winds and **earthquakes** are common there. People thought building a bridge there was impossible. But engineer Joseph Strauss disagreed. He told city leaders his idea in 1921. They thought about it for years.

The Golden Gate strait is 300 feet (91 m) deep.

JOSEPH STRAUSS

BORN: January 9, 1870, Cincinnati, Ohio

DIED: May 16, 1938, Los Angeles, California

Joseph Strauss was an engineer. He loved bridges. Strauss built more than 400 bridges! The Golden Gate Bridge was his most famous one. Strauss put together a strong team to build the bridge. He died soon after it was done.

BRIDGE DESIGN

City leaders approved Strauss's idea in 1930. Strauss got right to work. He hired other engineers. They helped design the bridge. He hired workers to construct it. The bridge was a **suspension bridge**. A tower was on each end. Cables ran between the towers. They held the road in place.

The main cables needed to be very strong. Each is more than three feet (0.9 m) in diameter.

THE TOWERS

Construction began in 1933. Workers built the towers first. They dug a pit. They poured concrete into it. This was the north tower's base. The south tower's base was built on the ocean floor. Workers used **explosives** to blow holes in the floor. Then they built a concrete base. Workers lowered it into the holes.

The tower base being built on the south shore of the Golden Gate

Steel beams were added once the bases were complete. These beams formed the towers. Each tower was 746 feet (227 m) above water!

CABLES AND NETS

In 1936, work began on the cables. Workers ran two main cables across the bridge. The cables were **flexible**. They allowed the bridge to sway. This would prevent **damage** during storms and **earthquakes**. Steel beams were hung from the cables.

Next, the bridge deck was built. Workers started at both ends. On November 18, the workers met in the middle. The deck was almost done!

Strauss wanted to keep workers safe. So a net was placed under the bridge.

PAINT AND PAVEMENT

The final step was **paving** the deck. Workers began this job in January 1937. They finished in April. Meanwhile, the bridge was painted. It was given a brand-new color. This color was called **international** orange. It helped the bridge stand out in fog. Ships were less likely to hit it.

Painting the bridge was a lot of work. Maintaining it is an ongoing job.

The bridge opened on May 27, 1937. It became an active route right away. It has been a busy bridge ever since!

TOURISM AND TRAVEL

The Golden Gate Bridge was an engineering marvel. It still is today! It is the world's ninth-longest **suspension bridge**.

The bridge is a San Francisco icon. It helps people travel quickly out of the city. More than 100,000 cars cross the bridge every day!

The bridge is a popular tourist site. Millions of people visit it each year.

BRIDGES OF THE WORLD

BROOKLYN BRIDGE

LOCATION: New York City

BUILT: 1883

CLEARANCE BELOW: 135 feet (41 m)

LENGTH: 1,595 feet (486 m)

BENEFITS: connects the **boroughs** of Brooklyn and Manhattan

TOWER BRIDGE

LOCATION: London, England

BUILT: 1894

CLEARANCE BELOW: 143 feet (44 m)

LENGTH: 800 feet (244 m)

BENEFITS: allows cars to cross the River Thames

The Golden Gate Bridge is just one of many awesome bridges. Check out these other cool bridges!

SYDNEY HARBOR BRIDGE
LOCATION: Sydney, Australia

BUILT: 1932

CLEARANCE BELOW: 161 feet (49 m)

LENGTH: 1,650 feet (503 m)

BENEFITS: crosses the Sydney Harbor, connecting the city of Sydney with smaller towns across the water

AKASHI STRAIT BRIDGE
LOCATION: Japan

BUILT: 1998

CLEARANCE BELOW: 213 feet (65 m)

LENGTH: 12,831 feet (3,911 m)

BENEFITS: crosses the Akashi **strait**, connecting the city islands of Honshu and Awaji

MORE ABOUT THE GOLDEN GATE BRIDGE

The Golden Gate Bridge was made to handle strong weather. It can withstand winds up to **100 MILES PER HOUR** (161 kmh)!

The bridge has only closed **THREE TIMES**. Each time was due to bad weather.

The safety net beneath the Golden Gate Bridge was important. It **SAVED 19 LIVES** during construction.

TEST YOUR KNOWLEDGE

1. Who was the engineer of the Golden Gate Bridge?

2. Construction on the Golden Gate Bridge began in 1933. TRUE OR FALSE?

3. How many feet high does each bridge tower rise above the water?

THINK ABOUT IT!

Are there any bridges near you? What do they cross?

GLOSSARY

borough – in some states, a town or area that has its own local government.

damage – to cause harm or ruin.

earthquake – when the ground shakes or trembles.

explosive – a substance used to cause an explosion.

flexible – easy to move or bend.

international (in-tuhr-NASH-nuhl) – of or relating to more than one nation.

pave – to cover a road surface with a hard material.

strait – a narrow waterway that connects two larger bodies of water.

suspension bridge – a bridge with a roadway that is held up by cables attached to tall towers.